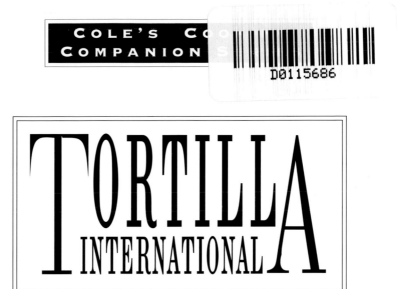

TORTILLA
INTERNATIONAL

COLE GROUP

© 1995 Cole Group, Inc.

Cover photograph: Patricia Brabant

Cole Group
1330 N. Dutton Ave., Suite 103
Santa Rosa, CA 95401
(800) 959-2717   (707) 526-2682
Fax (707) 526-2687

Printed in Hong Kong

G F E D C B A
1 0 9 8 7 6 5

ISBN 1-56426-803-9

Library of Congress Catalog Card Number 94-45540

Distributed to the book trade by Publishers Group West

Cole books are available for quantity purchases for sales promotions, premiums, fund-raising, or educational use. For more information on *Tortilla International* or other Cole's Cooking Companion books, please write or call the publisher.

CONTENTS

A New Approach to World Cuisine 5

Tortillas 6
Other World-Class Wrappers 7
Fillings for A New World Cuisine 8

Recipes and Techniques for the Tortilla International 11

World-Class Wrappers 12
Making Corn and Flour Tortillas 14
Garnishes for Tacos and Sopes 17
Making Sopes 19
Preparing Spring Rolls and Lumpia 23
Making Crêpes 27

Fillings and Accompaniments 28
Brown Bag Tortillas 30
Roasting and Peeling Chiles 32
The Well-Sauced Tortilla 37
Savory Crêpe Fillings 42

Traditional and Cross-Cultural Specialties 44
Making Tortilla Bowls 56
Preparing Tortillas for Tacos 64

Desserts 90
Crêpe Desserts 93

Index 95

A New Approach to World Cuisine

*T*he staple of both cuisine *mexicana* and
the cooking of the U.S. Southwest, the tortilla
has come to be the *compadre* of chefs and
home cooks from Santa Fe all the way
to Syracuse—and no wonder. Eaten plain or
wrapped around a variety of fillings, the tortilla
is versatile and convenient, the indispensable
foundation of many a delicious meal or snack.
As celebrated in *Tortilla International*, the
tortilla (and other world-class wrappers) form
the basis of a new world cuisine.

TORTILLAS

These thin rounds of corn or wheat that are the very heart of both traditional and contemporary Mexican cooking are truly multi-talented. Corn tortillas are made from *masa,* a dough prepared by grinding dried field corn that has been soaked in lime-treated water; flour tortillas are made from wheat.

Tortillas stack up nicely on the nutritional scale, with less than a gram of fat and no cholesterol (assuming they're made with vegetable oil, not lard). A corn tortilla has only about 60 calories; a flour tortilla, about 100.

When it comes to mouth-watering dishes with an international flavor, a dozen or so tortillas represents almost unlimited potential. Especially when they are freshly made (see pages 13–16), tortillas are good eaten plain, providing a welcome change from bread or crackers. Cut up and toasted or fried, they become *totopas*—crisp triangles for scooping up salsa and other foods. Dried and crumbled, they make a tasty thickener for soup, chili, or stew. And wrapped around a multitude of traditional fillings (see pages 29–33), tortillas are the basis of an astonishing assortment of Mexican specialties: tacos, burritos, tostadas, quesadillas, enchiladas, chimichangas, and more.

Tortillas are convenient to buy and store: Fresh and frozen corn and flour tortillas and pre-formed shells for tacos and tostadas are available in almost every supermarket and in Latin American markets. Compared to other convenience foods, tortillas are a bargain, especially when bought in quantity. They keep well for a week or two in the refrigerator and, tightly wrapped, for a couple of months in the freezer. *Masa harina,* a type of flour used to make corn tortillas, sopes, and other masa dishes, is also widely available and keeps well.

OTHER WORLD-CLASS WRAPPERS

Tortillas have a good deal in common with several other international wrappers of world-class fame: Mandarin pancakes, spring roll wrappers, chapatis, pita breads, and crêpes. Like the tortilla, most all these foods are staples of their native cuisines and have been absorbed into U.S. culinary culture. Available ready-made in supermarkets and specialty food stores, all these wrappers can be made at home (see pages 17–27). And like the tortilla, they can be combined with traditional fillings or with ones from a different culture to create an almost infinite variety of great-tasting dishes.

Mandarin Pancakes The ancestor of these Chinese flatbreads was a kind of noodle baked on a flat, heated stone. Served with mu shu-style dishes, they are popular take-out fare at Chinese restaurants. Frozen Mandarin pancakes are available in well-stocked supermarkets, and many Chinese markets sell freshly made ones.

Spring Roll Wrappers Used for making Chinese or Southeast Asian spring rolls and Philippine lumpia, these wrappers are of two basic types: One is square, made from a crêpe-like batter; the other is round, made of flour and water. They are available fresh and frozen in supermarkets and Asian markets.

Chapatis Similar in appearance to flour tortillas, chapatis are a staple bread in India and Sri Lanka, served with curries and other traditional fare. They are sold fresh in many supermarkets and natural food stores.

Pita Breads These yeasted flatbreads have a distinctive "pocket" that seems tailor-made for filling. In the Middle East they are used for scooping or dipping a variety of foods. Pita are sold in most supermarkets and natural food stores.

Crêpes Made to be filled, crêpes are prepared from a thin egg batter rather than from dough. In France, where they originated, they are served as a snack, lunch or supper dish, or even as dessert, depending upon how they are filled. In the U.S. crêpes are also popular at breakfast. Frozen crêpes are available in well-stocked supermarkets and specialty food stores.

FILLINGS FOR A NEW WORLD CUISINE

Whether the filling is a blend of exotic ingredients imported from the other side of the globe or a few well-chosen items pulled from the refrigerator or pantry, two qualities alone are essential: diversity and imagination. These are the distinguishing features of traditional wrapped and filled delicacies that are favorites the world over.

The collection of filling recipes beginning on page 28 is arranged by ethnic origin (Mexican, Asian, etc.). But given the diversity of combinations in the specialty recipe section (see pages 44–89), it's easy to see that most any filling can be paired with most any wrapper. Let the recipes and suggestions in *Tortilla International* spark your imagination as you create your own combinations for a new world cuisine.

RECIPES AND TECHNIQUES FOR THE TORTILLA INTERNATIONAL

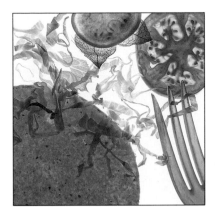

Something delicious wrapped around something equally delicious makes an irresistible package, whatever the culinary origins of the ingredients. Here are more than 50 recipes and basic techniques for imaginatively combining tortillas and other world-class wrappers with a variety of fillings and accompaniments. Simple or sophisticated, savory or sweet, geared to breakfast, lunch, supper, or in-between—the possibilities are unlimited.

WORLD-CLASS WRAPPERS

A stack of tortillas, spring roll wrappers, pita breads, crêpes, or other wrappers opens up a world of culinary possibilities. As convenient as ready-made wrappers are, they can't be quite as fresh or flavorful as homemade. In this section you'll discover how simple, satisfying, and economical it can be to make your own *Tortilla International* wrappers.

CORN TORTILLAS

Freshly made, warm corn tortillas are unbelievably good eaten plain or spread with butter. Combined with any of the traditional Mexican fillings on pages 29–33, they are the basis for tacos, enchiladas, and a multitude of other tortilla-based specialties. Masa harina, a type of "flour" used for making corn tortillas, is available throughout the United States (see page 6).

| 2 cups | masa harina | 500 ml |
| 1¼ cups | warm water | 300 ml |

1. Place the masa harina in a bowl. Gradually work the water into the masa harina, adding more if needed. Mix together well. Knead for 3–5 minutes, pushing hard with the heel of your hand. Keep the dough well wrapped while you make the tortillas, so that it does not dry out.

2. Heat a heavy skillet over medium-high heat. Break off a walnut-sized piece of dough and pat it 2–3 times to partially flatten. Press in a tortilla press as shown in steps 1 and 2 on page 14, or roll with a rolling pin between two sheets of plastic wrap. If proportions of masa harina to water are correct, the plastic will easily peel away from the dough. If the dough cracks at the edges, add a little more water and knead well. If the dough sticks to the plastic, add a little more masa harina and knead well. It takes a little practice to know how the dough should feel.

3. Place the tortilla on the heated, ungreased skillet. Cook until the edges begin to dry (about 30 seconds). Turn over and cook until lightly speckled on the underside (about 1 minute). Turn a second time and cook for an additional 30 seconds. The total cooking time will be 2–3 minutes, depending upon the thickness of the tortilla and the temperature of the pan. A well-made tortilla will usually puff up on the second turn.

4. Wrap the tortillas in a towel to keep them soft and warm.

Makes 12 tortillas.

Making Corn and Flour Tortillas

Corn tortillas are flattened in a press; flour tortillas are rolled out with a rolling pin. In Mexico, both corn and flour tortillas are baked on a metal or earthenware griddle called a comal, *but a heavy skillet works just as well. As the tortillas are cooked, wrap them in a towel to keep them soft and warm for serving. The process of making corn tortillas (see recipe on page 13) is somewhat different from that of making flour tortillas (see recipe on page 16).*

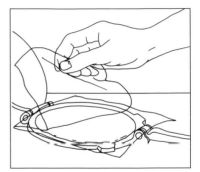

2. Open the press to reveal the flattened dough. Remove the plastic wrap from the tortilla and then lift the tortilla from the press. To cook corn tortillas, see Step 6 on page 15.

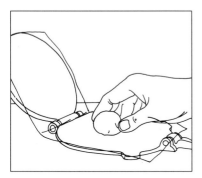

1. To shape corn tortillas, put a piece of plastic wrap on the surface of the tortilla press. Place a walnut-sized piece of masa slightly back of center on the press and cover with a piece of plastic wrap. Press down hard on the handle to flatten the masa.

3. To shape flour tortillas, squeeze a handful of dough so that a small ball of it extrudes from your fist. After balls are shaped, lightly coat each one with vegetable oil.

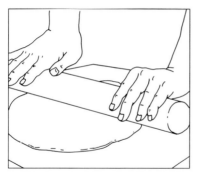

4. Lightly flour balls before rolling. Roll once forward and once back.

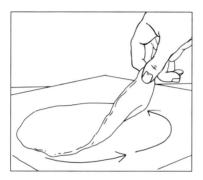

5. Flip tortilla and revolve a quarter turn. Keep rolling until desired size and thickness are achieved.

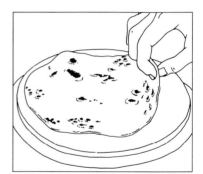

6. Use a hot, ungreased comal or heavy skillet to bake both corn and flour tortillas. Cook on both sides until speckled brown and cooked through.

FLOUR TORTILLAS

Flour tortillas are generally made a little larger than corn tortillas. Don't be discouraged if your first efforts are ragged and uneven (see photo on page 12.) Serve them warm, plain or with butter, or use them to make burritos, quesadillas, and chimichangas.

2 cups	flour	500 ml
scant 1 tsp	salt	scant 1 tsp
½ tsp	baking powder	½ tsp
¼ cup	shortening	60 ml
	or	
2 tbl	vegetable oil	2 tbl
½ cup	warm water	125 ml
as needed	vegetable oil	as needed

1. Mix together flour, salt, and baking powder. Cut in the shortening or oil and mix well. Gradually add the water, working it in to make a stiff dough. Knead until the dough is springy. Divide the dough into balls of equal size (see step 3 on page 14); Coat balls with oil, cover, and allow to rest for 20–30 minutes.

2. Heat a heavy skillet over medium-high heat. On a lightly floured board, use a rolling pin to roll each dough ball into a thin circle approximately 8 inches (20 cm) across.

3. Place the tortilla on the heated, ungreased skillet. Cook until speckled (1½–2 minutes); turn over and cook until the underside is speckled (1½–2 minutes). If the tortilla puffs up while cooking, press down lightly with a linen towel.

4. Wrap the tortillas in a towel to keep them soft and warm.

Makes 12 flour tortillas.

SOPES

Like tortillas, sopes are made from masa dough. These miniature pizza-like rounds are precooked and then fried just before being filled with beans, shredded meats, or other traditional Mexican tortilla fillings (see pages 29–33) and then garnished (see below).

¼ cup	shortening	60 ml
	or	
2 tbl	vegetable oil	2 tbl
2 cups	masa harina	500 ml
1¼ cups	warm water	300 ml

To prepare the shells with shortening, in a large mixing bowl, cream shortening; add masa harina alternately with water, mixing well after each addition. If using oil, combine the oil and water, then add slowly to masa harina, mixing well to make a soft dough. Divide the dough into 8 equal pieces. Shape and cook as directed on page 19.

Makes 8 sopes.

GARNISHES FOR TACOS AND SOPES

An assortment of garnishes is the crowning glory for tacos, sopes, and other filled masa dishes:

- *shredded iceberg lettuce or cabbage*
- *chopped onions (green, white, or red)*
- *sliced radishes*
- *guacamole (see page 33) or diced avocado*
- *chopped fresh mild or hot chiles*
- *grated cheese*
- *chopped cilantro (coriander leaves)*
- *salsa (see page 34)*

Making Sopes

Sopes, also referred to as gordas in some regions of Mexico and the Southwest, are easy to make when you follow the steps given here. The recipe for the dough is on page 17.

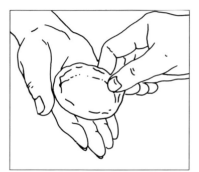

3. Pinch up the edges of each partially baked sope to form a rim about ⅝ inch (1.3 cm) high. This will hold the filling.

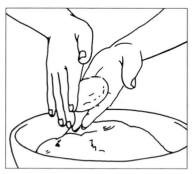

1. Moisten hands with water and form masa into walnut-size balls.

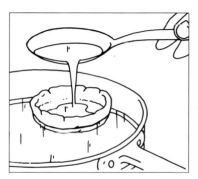

4. Fry sopes one at a time in hot oil until golden brown (about 4 minutes). Spoon hot oil into centers, turning once to cook top surface of sopes. Drain on paper towels before filling.

2. Pat balls into cakes about 3 inches (7.5 cm) across and ¼ inch (.6 cm) thick. Partially cook the cakes on a dry comal or an ungreased skillet, or bake in a 425°F (220°C) preheated oven for 12–15 minutes to set the dough.

MANDARIN PANCAKES

Also known as Peking doilies, these thin, soft flatbreads are the traditional Chinese accompaniment for mu shu pork (see page 72).

2 cups	flour	500 ml
¾ cup	boiling water	175 ml
2 tbl	peanut oil	2 tbl
1 tsp	sesame oil	1 tsp

1. Place flour in a bowl and add water gradually, stirring with a fork until dough holds together. Turn out onto a lightly floured board and knead until dough springs back (about 5 minutes). Dough should be slightly more moist and more dense than bread dough, but not sticky. Cover with plastic wrap and set aside to rest 30 minutes.

2. Roll dough into a 2-inch-diameter (5-cm) log. Cut in half and slice each half in half again, then divide each quarter into 4 even slices. Cover with a towel to prevent drying.

3. Heat a heavy skillet over medium-low heat. Oil surface lightly with 1 tablespoon of the peanut oil, and wipe away excess with a paper towel. Combine remaining peanut oil with sesame oil and set aside.

4. Flatten a piece of dough with the heel of your hand and roll into a 3-inch (7.5-cm) circle. Repeat with second piece of dough. Brush the tops lightly with oil mixture and lay one piece on top of the other, oiled sides together. Roll out to a diameter of 6 inches (15 cm). Place the pair of pancakes in hot skillet, oiled sides together, and cook until lightly blistered but not browned (about 45 seconds per side). Roll out next pair.

5. Remove cooked pancakes to a plate and cover with a towel to keep warm. After they have cooled for 1–2 minutes, peel each of the pairs apart. (Pancakes can be prepared up to this point several hours ahead of use.) Continue rolling and cooking remaining dough. Steam for 10 minutes before serving.

Makes 16 pancakes.

Spring Roll Wrappers I

This homemade Asian-style wrapper is made with egg; the version below contains no egg. Both can be used interchangeably for spring rolls or Philippine lumpia (see pages 36–37, 76, and 78).

1	egg	1
½ cup plus 2 tbl	water	125 ml plus 2 tbl
⅔ cup	cornstarch	150 ml
pinch	salt	pinch

Combine ingredients and stir until smooth; let stand 15 minutes. Lightly oil an 8-inch (20-cm) nonstick skillet or crêpe pan over medium heat. Pour a scant 2 tablespoons batter into pan and quickly tilt and swirl to cover bottom with batter. Cook until edges begin to peel away from pan (about 1 minute). Lift edge with fingertips or spatula, turn, cook 30 seconds on second side, and turn out onto a plate. Continue with remaining batter.

Makes 8 wrappers.

Spring Roll Wrappers II

This dough makes an especially delicate wrapper.

1¼ cups	water	300 ml
1 cup	cake flour, sifted	250 ml
pinch	salt	pinch

Combine ingredients and stir until smooth; let stand 15 minutes. Batter should have the consistency of thick cream. Preheat and oil skillet as above, but instead of pouring batter into pan, brush it on with a wide pastry brush, adding a second or third coat as necessary to fill in gaps and thin spots. Cook as directed above.

Makes 8 wrappers.

Preparing Spring Rolls and Lumpia

Depending upon the type of filling you use, fry the prepared rolls or serve without additional cooking (see pages 36–37, 76, and 78). Use either of the dough recipes on the opposite page, then follow these steps:

2. Roll wrapper partly around filling, tuck in edges; continue rolling.

1. Place filling near one edge of the wrapper, leaving space on both ends to seal ends of roll.

3. Moisten tip of wrapper with beaten egg to seal. Briefly sauté rolls, sealed side down, in a small amount of hot oil to ensure a good seal before serving or deep-frying.

CHAPATIS

The chapati, the tortilla of India and neighboring Sri Lanka (formerly Ceylon), is a traditional accompaniment for Sri Lankan Curry (see page 84). Similar in appearance and flavor to a flour tortilla, the chapati also makes a tasty wrapper for any Mexican filling (see pages 29–33).

1 cup	whole wheat flour	250 ml
¼ tsp	salt	¼ tsp
1 tbl	oil	1 tbl
¼–⅓ cup	water	60–85 ml

1. In a large bowl, combine the flour, salt and oil. Rub the oil into the flour until evenly distributed throughout. Add ¼ cup (60 ml) of the water and knead the mixture in the bowl to form a thick dough. If the mixture is too crumbly, add more water, ½ tablespoon at a time, until it is the proper consistency.

2. Transfer to lightly oiled surface and knead for 10–15 minutes, or until dough is stiff but smooth. Form into a ball and divide into 6 balls of equal size.

3. Press ball flat between your palms. On a lightly floured board, roll each flattened ball into a 6-inch-diameter (15-cm) circle.

4. Heat a heavy skillet over medium heat and place chapati in it. Cook on the first side for 30 seconds, then turn and cook on the second side 30 seconds. Turn again, pressing lightly on the chapati. The chapati should puff at this point. Turn the chapati over again and continue to cook and turn a few more times until lightly browned on both sides.

5. Remove from the pan and repeat with remaining dough.

Makes 6 chapatis.

PITA BREAD

Serve pita breads with hummus (see page 41) or top them with anything you would put on a pizza crust.

1 tbl	active dry yeast	1 tbl
1½ cups	lukewarm water	350 ml
1 tbl	honey	1 tbl
3 cups	unbleached flour	700 ml
1 tsp	salt	1 tsp
as needed	oil, for bowl	as needed
as needed	yellow cornmeal	as needed

1. In a large bowl, sprinkle yeast over water, stir in honey and let stand 5 minutes. Beat in 1¾ cups (425 ml) flour. Beat vigorously until bubbles form. Beat in salt and remaining flour to form stiff dough. Turn out onto floured surface and knead, adding more flour as needed to prevent sticking, until dough is smooth and pliable (about 5 minutes). Form into smooth ball, place in oiled bowl, turn to coat all surfaces, cover with towel, and let rise in warm place until doubled (about 1 hour).

2. Punch down, cover, and let rise a second time until doubled in bulk. Punch down, knead briefly and divide into 10 pieces. Knead each piece briefly and form into a ball. Cover with towel and let rise 20–30 minutes.

3. Preheat oven to 500°F (260°C). Keeping remaining dough covered, roll 1 ball at a time into a 6-inch (15-cm) circle approximately ⅛ inch (.3 cm) thick and place on surface lightly dusted with cornmeal. Cover with towel and repeat with remaining balls.

4. When first 2 circles have rested 10 minutes, quickly transfer to oven and bake for 5–8 minutes directly on the floor of the oven or on a heavy baking sheet on the lowest oven rack, until pita breads are golden and puff. Remove to wire rack to cool. Repeat with remaining circles, baking 2 at a time.

Makes 10 pita breads.

Basic Crêpes

These can be folded, rolled, or wrapped around a variety of savory or sweet fillings (see pages 42 and 93). To make a simple dessert crêpe, add 2 tablespoons granulated or brown sugar to the liquid ingredients before blending with flour. Crêpes will keep up to 5 days in the refrigerator or up to 2 months in the freezer; to store, layer cooled crêpes between pieces of waxed paper and wrap with aluminum foil. Allow crêpes to warm to room temperature before using.

¾ cup	milk	175 ml
¾ cup	water	175 ml
4	eggs	4
⅛ tsp	salt	⅛ tsp
¼ cup	butter, melted	60 ml
1 cup	flour	250 ml
¼ cup	oil, for cooking	60 ml

1. In 2-quart (1.8-l) bowl, thoroughly combine milk, water, eggs, salt, and melted butter. Blend in flour to form a smooth batter. Let batter rest 30 minutes to allow the flour to absorb the liquid. The batter should thicken to the consistency of whipping cream.

2. Heat a 6-inch-diameter (15-cm) crêpe pan or heavy skillet over medium-high heat until smoking hot. Lower heat slightly and brush interior surface of pan with oil. Spoon 3–4 tablespoons batter into pan, quickly swirling batter to coat bottom of pan. Pour any excess batter back into bowl.

3. Cook only until crêpe is dry and slightly browned (about 1 minute). Turn crêpe over and cook second side 30 seconds. Remove to a plate to cool completely.

4. Repeat procedure with remaining batter, brushing pan with oil as needed.

Makes about 20 crêpes.

MAKING CRÊPES

A proper crêpe pan is made of rolled steel or lined copper, with flaring sides and a flat, well-defined bottom to give the crêpe a sharp edge. Reserve the pan strictly for crêpes and you will never need to wash it; simply wipe it clean with a paper towel dipped in a little oil and store in a dry place.

2. Turn crêpe with metal spatula (when bottom is browned). Lightly brown other side (about 30 seconds).

1. Heat 6-inch (15-cm) crêpe pan over medium-high heat until smoking hot. Reduce heat and brush pan with ¼ teaspoon oil. Pour 3–4 tablespoons of batter into center of pan. Gently tilt pan so batter coats entire surface. Cook crêpe about 60 seconds or until it begins to bubble.

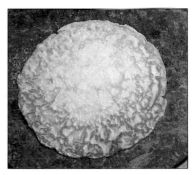

3. Transfer crêpe to a plate and fill as desired (see pages 42 and 93).

FILLINGS AND ACCOMPANIMENTS

Perfectly seasoned morsels of meat, seafood, vegetables, and fruits in edible wrappers are perennial favorites the world over. This section presents a variety of fillings and accompaniments you can use to prepare a global feast of well-filled, well-sauced delicacies from Mexico, Asia, and other locales famous for their filled specialties.

Picadillo Filling

Picadillo is Spanish for "minced" or "chopped." Using ground beef won't produce the authentic texture of this traditional Mexican filling for tacos and sopes, but the flavor will be almost as good. The addition of fresh apples and raisins makes a refreshing combination of spicy and sweet flavors.

1 lb	lean beef, coarsely chopped	450 g
2 tbl	oil	2 tbl
1	onion, diced	1
1 clove	garlic, minced	1 clove
2	tomatoes, chopped	2
1	apple, peeled, cored, and chopped	1
¼ cup	seedless raisins, plumped in hot water and drained	60 ml
⅛ tsp	ground cinnamon	⅛ tsp
pinch each	ground cloves and ground cumin	pinch each
½ cup	water	125 ml
to taste	salt	to taste

1. Sauté meat in the oil until browned. Add onion and garlic and cook until soft.

2. Add tomatoes, apple, raisins, cinnamon, cloves, cumin, and water. Simmer until liquid is absorbed (about 25 minutes). Check the seasoning and salt to taste.

Makes about 4 cups (900 ml).

MACHACA FILLING

This is a classic filling for burritos, tacos, chimichangas, and flautas.

1 lb	chuck roast, cut into 2-inch (5-cm) cubes	450 g
½	onion, chopped	½
1 clove	garlic, minced	1 clove
2 tbl	oil	2 tbl
3	tomatoes, chopped	3
2	canned or roasted jalapeño chiles, chopped (see page 32)	2
to taste	salt	to taste
3	eggs, beaten	3

1. Place meat in a pot and cover with cold water. Bring to a boil, cover, and simmer until tender, 1–1½ hours. Allow the meat to cool in its own broth until easy to handle. Shred the meat by using your fingers, two forks, or a food processor using the plastic blade. (Place a few pieces at a time into the container and process briefly.) Avoid shredding the meat too fine.

2. Sauté onion and garlic in the oil until the onion is soft. Add tomatoes and chiles and cook until the tomatoes are soft. Mix in the meat, check the seasoning, and salt to taste.

3. Lower the heat and add the beaten eggs. Stir to break up the eggs; cook until the eggs are set.

Makes about 4 cups (900 ml).

BROWN BAG TORTILLAS

With a little imagination, you can pack a terrific brown bag lunch with a southwestern flavor. Pack a small microwave-safe container with canned refried beans or any of the Mexican fillings on pages 29–33. Pack a second container with your favorite garnishes for tacos or sopes (see page 17). Slip one or two tortillas into a lock-top bag and tuck it all into a lunch bag. At lunchtime, warm the filling, spoon it into the tortilla, add garnishes, and enjoy!

Puerco Filling

This recipe using ground pork provides a simple, quick filling with good texture and authentic Mexican flavor. It is especially good for sopes, tacos, flautas, burritos, and chimichangas. The mild poblano chile is known as ancho when dried.

1	dried ancho chile	1
½ cup	boiling water	125 ml
1	tomato, chopped	1
1 lb	ground pork	450 g
1	onion, chopped	1
1 clove	garlic, minced	1 clove
1 can (4 oz)	diced green chiles	1 can (115 g)
½ tsp	dried oregano	½ tsp
¼ tsp	ground cumin	¼ tsp
to taste	salt	to taste
1	potato, cooked, peeled, and diced	1

1. Remove seeds and veins from ancho chile. Wash ancho and soak in boiling water for 30 minutes. Place the ancho, water, and tomato into a blender or food processor and purée until smooth.

2. Crumble pork into a skillet and cook until browned (about 20 minutes) over medium high heat. Add onion and garlic and cook until soft. Add the diced green chiles, oregano, and cumin. Stir in the ancho-tomato purée, check the seasoning, and salt to taste.

3. Add potato and heat, stirring occasionally, until the potato is heated through.

Makes about 4 cups (900 ml).

CHICKEN-TOMATILLO FILLING

Use this easy-to-make shredded chicken and tomatillo filling for burritos, tacos, flautas, chimichangas, enchiladas, and sopes, or to stuff pita bread.

1	onion, chopped	1
2 cloves	garlic, minced	2 cloves
2 tbl	oil	2 tbl
1 can (12 oz)	tomatillos, drained and mashed	1 can (350 g)
½ tsp	salt	½ tsp
3 cups	cooked and shredded chicken	700 ml
¼ cup	cilantro (coriander leaves), coarsely chopped	60 ml

1. In a skillet sauté onion and garlic in the oil and cook until soft. Add tomatillos and salt. Bring to a boil, reduce heat, and cook 5 minutes to reduce the liquid.

2. Add chicken and cilantro and cook for 10 minutes more.

Makes about 4 cups (900 ml).

ROASTING AND PEELING CHILES

The distinctive flavor of roasted chiles gives authentic taste and texture to traditional Mexican dishes like the Pescado Filling on the opposite page.

1. Blister chile pod over a burner covered with a metal screen. Turn frequently with tongs. The chiles are done when the skins are charred and blistered. Some parts of the chile will be black. Take care not to burn through to the flesh. Place blistered chiles in a plastic bag to steam for 20 minutes.

2. When chiles are cool, hold them under cool water and peel the skin from the chile, starting from the stem end.

3. With a small, sharp knife, cut open the chile. Remove the veins and seeds. Wash out the last of the seeds under running water.

QUICK GUACAMOLE

Guacamole is used as a garnish for tacos, burritos, tostadas, or flautas, as well as a dip with tortilla chips or fresh vegetables. (See photo on page 35.)

2	avocados	2
⅓ cup	red or green salsa (see page 34)	85 ml
1	tomato, diced	1
¼	onion, finely minced	¼

Halve the avocados; remove seed, scoop out pulp, and mash with a fork. Combine with remaining ingredients and mix well. Serve at once.

Makes about 2 cups (500 ml).

PESCADO FILLING

This elegant fish filling can be used for flautas or tacos, as well as crêpes.

2 lb	firm ocean fish fillets, cut into bite-sized pieces	900 g
¼ cup	olive oil	60 ml
1	onion, chopped	1
2 cloves	garlic, minced	2 cloves
3	tomatoes, chopped	3
3	fresh poblano chiles, roasted, peeled, seeded, and chopped (see opposite page)	3
to taste	salt	to taste

In a medium-hot skillet sauté the fish in olive oil until it is tender and it flakes easily. Add onion and garlic and cook until soft. Add tomatoes and chiles and cook until soft. Check the seasoning and salt to taste, if necessary.

Makes about 4 cups (900 ml).

Salsa Azteca

This red table salsa is chunky and quite hot.

3	fresh or canned jalapeño chiles, minced	3
5	tomatoes, peeled and finely chopped	5
2 cloves	garlic, minced	2 cloves
1	white onion, minced	1
1 tbl	vinegar	1 tbl
2 tbl	cilantro (corander leaves), chopped	2 tbl
to taste	salt	to taste

In a bowl mix together chiles, tomatoes, garlic, onion, and vinegar. Stir in the cilantro and salt. Store tightly covered in the refrigerator for up to one week.

Makes 4 cups (900 ml).

Salsa Verde

This smooth, green salsa has an unusually fresh flavor and is particularly good with pork, chicken, and fish fillings for tacos or sopes.

1	fresh or canned jalapeño chile, chopped	1
1 can (12 oz)	tomatillos, drained	1 can (350 g)
2 cloves	garlic, chopped	2 cloves
3 tbl	finely minced onion	3 tbl
¼ cup	cilantro (coriander leaves)	60 ml
¼ tsp	salt	¼ tsp
¼ cup	water	60 ml

Place chiles, tomatillos, garlic, onion, cilantro, and salt in a blender or food processor and blend briefly to a purée. Add the water in small amounts and blend to the desired consistency.

Makes about 1½ cups (350 ml).

SPRING ROLL OR LUMPIA FILLING

This hot, spicy Asian filling must be fried after it is wrapped.

2 tbl	oil	2 tbl
¼ cup	water	60 ml
1	onion, minced	1
6 cloves	garlic, minced	6 cloves
1 tbl	finely minced fresh hot chiles	1 tbl
1 scant tsp	grated fresh ginger	1 scant tsp
½ lb	ground pork	225 g
½	red bell pepper, minced	½
½ cup	chopped fresh bean sprouts	125 ml
½ cup	finely shredded Chinese cabbage	125 ml
¼ cup	minced celery	60 ml
3	green onions, minced	3
1 tbl	minced fresh parsley	1 tbl
½ tsp	dry mustard	½ tsp
2 tbl	soy sauce	2 tbl
1½ tsp	sugar	1½ tsp
to taste	coarsely ground black pepper and salt	to taste
1 cup	finely shredded cooked chicken	250 ml
2	eggs, lightly beaten	2
1 cup	mashed potatoes	250 ml

1. Heat the oil and water over high heat in a wok. Add the onion, garlic, chiles, and ginger and stir-fry for about 2 minutes. Add all the remaining ingredients except the chicken, eggs, and potatoes. Stir-fry for another 2–3 minutes or until vegetables are wilted but not overcooked. Remove from the heat and add the cooked chicken. Stir the eggs into the mixture.

2. Spread wrapper thinly and evenly with the mashed potato, leaving a ½-inch (1.25-cm) margin all around the edge. Then fill with pork and vegetable mixture and seal as described on page 23.

3. To fry, proceed as for Lumpia Shanghai (see page 78).

Makes about 6 cups (1.4 l).

Imperial Asian Filling

This filling can be wrapped in spring roll wrappers or flour tortillas and served with Nuoc Mam Sauce (see page 38). Like the filling on the opposite page, it must be cooked after being wrapped. Look for the bean thread noodles and cloud ear mushrooms in Asian markets.

1½ oz	bean thread noodles	45 g
⅓ lb	finely ground pork, cooked	150 g
¼ lb	cooked crabmeat or minced cooked shrimp	115 g
1 tbl	cloud ear mushrooms, soaked, drained, and finely shredded	1 tbl
½ cup	minced green or yellow onion	125 ml
1 clove	garlic, minced	1 clove
pinch	freshly ground black pepper	pinch

1. Soak bean threads in water until soft. Drain and cut into 1-inch (2.5-cm) lengths. Combine with pork, mushrooms, onion, garlic, and pepper and blend thoroughly.

2. Wrap and seal according to instructions on page 23. To fry, proceed as for Lumpia Shanghai (see page 78).

Makes about 3 cups (700 ml).

The Well-Sauced Tortilla

The mild flavor of tortillas, chapatis, and other international wrappers provides a perfect backdrop for highly flavored sauces:

- *chile-spiked salsas (see page 34) to complement Mexican fillings*

- *fiery Berberé Sauce (see page 39) to heat up stews like Sik Sik Wat (see page 85)*

- *traditional hot and sweet table sauces (see page 38) to add authentic sparkle to Asian wrapped delicacies*

Nuoc Mam Sauce

This Vietnamese sauce (see photo on opposite page) emphasizes the flavor of the bottled fish sauce, available in Asian markets.

1 clove	garlic	1 clove
1 small	green chile, minced	1 small
3 tbl	bottled fish sauce	3 tbl
1 tsp	vinegar or lime juice	1 tsp
1 tsp	sugar	1 tsp
1 tbl	water	1 tbl

To prepare in a mortar, pound garlic and chile together, then blend in remaining ingredients. To prepare in a blender or food processor, combine all ingredients and blend thoroughly.

Makes ⅓ cup (85 ml).

Sweet Lumpia Sauce

Use with lumpia as a dipping sauce (see pages 76 and 78) or to add zip to burritos made with Asian fillings (see pages 72 and 74).

1 cup	chicken stock or meat broth	250 ml
⅓ cup	brown sugar	85 ml
4 cloves	garlic, crushed	4 cloves
1½ tsp	cornstarch	1½ tsp
2 tbl	soy sauce	2 tbl
to taste	bottled hot-pepper sauce	to taste

In a small saucepan combine broth, sugar, and garlic and bring to a boil, stirring to dissolve sugar. Cook to reduce mixture by one third. Mix cornstarch into soy sauce, stirring until dissolved. Stir cornstarch mixture into sauce and cook until thickened and glossy. Add a few drops of hot-pepper sauce.

Makes ¾ cup (175 ml).

BERBERÉ SAUCE

A hot, hot seasoning paste used with African fare such as Sik Sik Wat (see page 85), this spicy condiment can put a bit of fire in Mexican or Asian specialties as well.

3–4	tomatoes, coarsely chopped	3–4
1 tbl	grated fresh ginger	1 tbl
3–4	fresh hot chiles, minced	3–4
¼ tsp each	ground coriander, cardamom, fenugreek, nutmeg, and cinnamon	¼ tsp each
pinch	ground cloves	pinch
1	onion, minced	1
4–5 cloves	garlic, minced	4–5 cloves
1½ tsp	salt	1½ tsp
¼ cup	dry red wine	60 ml
1 cup	paprika	250 ml
2–3 tbl	cayenne	2–3 tbl
½ tsp	coarsely ground black pepper	½ tsp
2 tbl	oil	2 tbl
1½ tbl	sugar	1½ tbl
1 tbl	minced fresh cilantro (coriander leaves)	1 tbl

Put all ingredients in a saucepan and cook over medium heat, stirring constantly, until a thick sauce results (about 15–20 minutes). Transfer to a jar, cool, and refrigerate for up to 3 weeks.

Makes about 1½ cups (350 ml).

GREEK SALAD FILLING

Halve a pita and spread with Hummus, then top it with this salad to make a refreshing, healthy lunch or snack (see recipe and photo on opposite page).

2	green bell peppers	2
1	cucumber	1
3	tomatoes	3
2 stalks	celery	2 stalks
¼ lb	feta cheese	115 g
½	red onion, diced	½
½ tsp	salt	½ tsp
to taste	freshly ground black pepper	to taste
3 tbl	vinegar	3 tbl
¼ cup	oil	60 ml
½ tsp	oregano	½ tsp
1 tbl	fresh basil, minced	1 tbl

1. Seed peppers and cut into 1-inch (2.5-cm) squares. Peel cucumber and cut into 1-inch (2.5-cm) cubes. Cut tomatoes into 1-inch (2.5-cm) cubes. Slice celery on the diagonal into ½-inch-thick (1.25-cm) pieces. Cut feta cheese into ½-inch (1.25-cm) cubes.

2. In a 2-quart (1.8-l) bowl, mix peppers, cucumber, tomatoes, celery, feta cheese, and red onion. Season with salt, pepper, vinegar, oil, oregano, and basil.

Makes about 4 cups (900 ml).

HUMMUS

Garbanzo beans, or chick-peas, have one of the highest protein contents of any of the legumes. Puréed with tahini (sesame butter), they make a luscious Middle Eastern spread for pita breads, tortillas, or chapatis. Tahini is available at most supermarkets and natural food stores. Hummus will keep for about a week in the refrigerator.

1	lemon, juiced	1
1 can (15¼ oz)	cooked garbanzo beans, drained	1 can (435 g)
2 cloves	garlic, minced	2 cloves
2 tbl	tahini	2 tbl
⅛ tsp	salt	⅛ tsp

In a blender or food processor, combine lemon juice, garbanzo beans, garlic, tahini, and salt. Blend to a smooth paste.

Makes 1¾ cups (425 ml).

Savory Crêpe Fillings

A stack of crêpes and a savory filling makes a quick but elegant brunch, lunch, or supper dish.

Sausage and Spinach Crêpes *This crêpe is assembled after cooking, unlike the ones that follow. Heat a package of frozen creamed spinach. Place a dollop of creamed spinach in center of crêpe. Top with cooked and browned Polish sausage slices, and fold in edges of crêpe toward the center to make a square (see opposite page).*

The following crêpes are assembled as the crêpe is cooking. After turning the crêpe, add one of the following fillings, fold in half, and remove from pan to plate:

Cheese and Bacon Crêpes *Fill crêpe with grated Gruyère cheese and crumbled bacon.*

Chicken-Liver Crêpes *Fill with sliced sautéed chicken livers seasoned with freshly ground black pepper. Top with a dollop of sour cream and a sliced ripe olive.*

Ham and Cheese Crêpes *Fill crêpe with paper-thin slices of Gruyère cheese and cooked ham.*

Mexican Crêpes *Fill crêpe with a spoonful of any of the Mexican fillings on pages 29–33. Drizzle red or green salsa over the crêpe just before serving, if desired.*

Mushroom Crêpes *Fill crêpe with sliced sautéed mushrooms and drizzle folded crêpe with Crème Fraîche or sour cream.*

Princess Crêpes *Fill with steamed fresh asparagus tips and sliced raw mushrooms that have been sprinkled with fresh lemon juice.*

Provençale Crêpes *Fill with diced fresh tomato and a pinch of minced garlic. Sprinkle minced parsley over the crêpe just before serving, if desired.*

Smoked Salmon Crêpes *Fill with strips of thinly sliced smoked salmon (lox). Add a sprinkling of lemon juice and top with chopped chives.*

TRADITIONAL AND CROSS-CULTURAL SPECIALTIES

This section reflects traditional pairings of wrappers and fillings as well as innovative cross-cultural combinations that bring together a wrapper from one part of the globe and a filling from another. Whether you prefer conventional or multi-ethnic combinations, you will find recipes and suggestions here that underscore the diversity—and fun—of a new approach to world cuisine.

SPICY CRABMEAT TOSTADAS

Great for a quick meal, these light and healthy tostadas are baked rather than deep-fried. Make the filling ahead and top the tostadas right before serving.

¼ cup	minced red onion	60 ml
1 tsp	oil	1 tsp
½ tsp	minced garlic	½ tsp
1 cup	diced tomatoes	250 ml
2 tbl	minced cilantro (coriander leaves)	2 tbl
2 cups	cooked crabmeat, shredded	500 ml
6	corn tortillas	6
2 tbl	lemon juice	2 tbl
¼ cup	chopped green bell pepper	60 ml
¼ cup	peeled and chopped cucumber	60 ml
1 cup	shredded lettuce	250 ml
as needed	salsa (see page 34)	as needed

1. Preheat oven to 350°F (175°C). In a large skillet over medium-high heat, sauté onion in oil until soft (about 3 minutes). Add garlic, tomatoes, cilantro, and crabmeat. Cook for 5 minutes.

2. Bake corn tortillas in oven until crisp (about 7–10 minutes). In a large bowl mix together lemon juice, bell pepper, cucumber, and lettuce. Place equal amounts of lettuce mixture on tostadas, then top with crab mixture. Serve immediately with salsa.

Serves 6.

CHICKEN MOLE TORTA

This layered chocolate-scented dish is perfect for special occasions.

3–5	dried New Mexico chiles	3–5
2 tbl	oil	2 tbl
1	onions, diced	1
1 clove	garlic, minced	1 clove
¾ tsp	salt	¾ tsp
1½ tsp	ground cinnamon	1½ tsp
⅛ cup	raisins	30 ml
¼ tsp	cumin seed	¼ tsp
⅛ cup	minced cilantro (coriander leaves)	30 ml
¼ oz	unsweetened chocolate	8 g
1½ cups	chicken stock	350 ml
4 cups	shredded, cooked chicken	900 ml
¼ cup	whole almonds, toasted and coarsely ground	60 ml
7	flour tortillas (10-inch or 25-cm diameter)	7
1 cup	warm refried beans	250 ml
1 cup	Quick Guacamole (see page 33)	250 ml
¼ cup	grated Monterey jack cheese	60 ml
as needed	salsa, for garnish (see page 34)	as needed
1 cup	sour cream, for garnish	250 ml
8 sprigs	cilantro (coriander leaves), for garnish	8 sprigs

1. Place chiles in a bowl and cover with boiling water. Let soak 30 minutes. Remove and cut in thin strips. Reserve 1 cup (250 ml) soaking liquid.

2. In a large saucepan place oil, onions, and garlic and cook until softened (7–8 minutes). Stir in chile strips, reserved soaking liquid, salt, cinnamon, raisins, cumin seed, cilantro, chocolate, and chicken stock. Bring to a boil, reduce heat, and simmer for 30 minutes. Add chicken and 3 tablespoons ground almonds and stir to thicken.

3. Preheat oven to 375°F (190°C). To assemble torta, place a tortilla on an ovenproof serving dish. Spread with half the chicken mixture. Top with another tortilla. Spread with ½ cup

(125 ml) refried beans, top with another tortilla, and spread
with half the guacamole. Repeat layers, top with a tortilla, and
sprinkle with grated cheese.

4. Bake torta until piping hot and cheese has melted (about
   20 minutes). To serve, cut into 8 wedges, and sprinkle with
   remaining almonds. Garnish with salsa, sour cream, and
   cilantro sprigs.

Serves 8.

New Mexico-Style Beef Burritos

Burritos are simply warmed tortillas filled with beans, meat, or some other Mexican filling (see pages 29–33). After filling, they can be eaten as is, baked briefly in a 450°F (230°C) oven, or grilled over hot coals.

1 lb	ground beef	450 g
1	onion, chopped	1
1 can (16 oz)	refried beans	1 can (450 g)
1 can (8 oz)	stewed tomatoes	1 can (225 g)
⅓ cup	hot or mild salsa	85 ml
1 cup	sliced ripe olives	250 ml
as needed	canned or fresh diced green chiles	as needed
as needed	sliced jalapeño chiles	as needed
1 tsp each	chili powder and salt	1 tsp each
4	large flour tortillas, warmed (see Note)	4
1 cup	shredded Cheddar or Monterey jack cheese	250 ml
as needed	salsa, for garnish	as needed
as needed	avocado slices, for garnish	as needed
as needed	cherry tomatoes, for garnish	as needed
as needed	hot chiles, for garnish	as needed

1. In a large skillet, sauté ground beef and onion until meat is browned and onion is soft.

2. Stir in refried beans, stewed tomatoes, salsa, olives, chiles, chili powder, and salt. Heat until bubbly.

3. Place about ½ cup (125 ml) of filling down the center of each tortilla; top with a sprinkling of cheese. Fold top and bottom edges over filling, and then fold in sides.

4. Garnish as desired with salsa, avocado, tomatoes, and hot chiles.

Serves 4.

Note *To warm tortillas, wrap in foil and place in 350°F (175°C) oven for 10 minutes.*

SHRIMP BURRITOS CANCÚN

Seafood fillings are popular along the Mexican coast.

1¼ lb	shrimp, boiled and shelled	570 g
1 tbl	lime juice	1 tbl
¼ cup	minced onion	60 ml
1 cup	chopped tomatillos, canned or freshly cooked	250 ml
½	serrano or jalapeño chile, minced	½
⅛ cup	minced cilantro (coriander leaves)	30 ml
1 clove	garlic, minced	1 clove
1	ripe avocado, peeled and seeded	1
¼ tsp	ground cumin	¼ tsp
1 tbl	minced green onion	1 tbl
to taste	salt	to taste
2 cups	shredded iceberg or romaine lettuce	500 ml
as needed	lime wedges, for garnish	as needed
as needed	cilantro (coriander leaves), for garnish	as needed
6	large flour tortillas	6
as needed	sour cream, for garnish	as needed

1. Cut shrimp into large chunks. Place in a large bowl and add 1½ teaspoons of the lime juice; toss.

2. In a food processor or blender, in batches if necessary, combine onion, tomatillos, chiles, 1 tablespoon of the cilantro, garlic, and avocado. Blend briefly; mixture should be slightly chunky. Transfer to a bowl and stir in remaining ½ tablespoon lime juice, cumin, remaining cilantro, green onion, and salt. Cover and chill avocado sauce until ready to serve.

3. Mound lettuce on a large platter. Top with shrimp. Garnish with lime wedges and cilantro. Cover and chill up to 2 hours; remove from refrigerator 30 minutes before serving.

4. Heat tortillas briefly. To serve, place hot tortillas in a towel lined-basket next to lettuce-lined shrimp platter, a bowl of the avocado sauce, and a bowl of sour cream.

Serves 6.

ENCHILADAS COLORADAS

Enchiladas are "chilied" corn tortillas. After filling, they can be rolled, stacked, or folded.

1 recipe	Mexican filling (see pages 29–33)	1 recipe
1 can (6 oz)	tomato sauce	1 can (170 g)
2 cloves	garlic, chopped	2 cloves
1 tsp	dried oregano	1 tsp
½ tsp	ground cumin	½ tsp
¼ tsp	ground cloves	¼ tsp
3 tbl	oil	3 tbl
1 tbl	flour	1 tbl
1 can (10 oz)	enchilada sauce	1 can (285 g)
as needed	oil, for frying	as needed
12	corn tortillas	12
2 cups	grated longhorn, Colby, or jack cheese	500 ml
as needed	sour cream and chopped green onion, for garnish	as needed
as needed	cilantro (coriander leaves)	as needed
as needed	black olives, for garnish	as needed

1. Prepare filling and set aside. Place the tomato sauce, garlic, oregano, cumin, and cloves in a blender or food processor, and blend briefly.

2. In a skillet heat the oil over medium heat, add flour, and lightly brown, stirring. Add the tomato purée and fry for 3 minutes, stirring constantly. Slowly stir in the enchilada sauce. Bring to a boil, stirring constantly; reduce heat and simmer 5 minutes. Keep warm.

3. Preheat oven to 350°F (175°C). Heat oil in a skillet over high heat to 400°F (205°C). Fry each tortilla, one at a time, long enough to soften it (a few seconds per side). Remove with tongs and dip it into the warm sauce. Coat both sides of tortilla; then remove to a plate. Place some of the prepared filling across the middle of the tortilla, fold over, and place in a baking pan. Repeat until all tortillas are filled.

4. Spoon remaining sauce over enchiladas. Sprinkle the grated cheese over the enchiladas, cover the pan tightly with foil, and bake until enchiladas are heated through and cheese has melted (20–30 minutes). Garnish with sour cream, green onion, cilantro, and olives before serving.

Makes 12 enchiladas.

Ensenada Enchiladas

This easy-to-fix Mexican entrée can be prepared ahead to heat in the oven at serving time. Serve with corn salsa or your favorite tomato salsa and mineral water (or a margarita) to round out the meal.

12	flour tortillas	12
2 cans (15 oz each)	enchilada sauce	2 cans (430 g each)
6 cups	warm refried beans	1.4 l
2 cups	Monterey jack cheese, shredded	500 ml
1½ cups	Salsa Azteca (see page 34)	350 ml
1 recipe	Quick Guacamole (see page 33)	1 recipe

1. Preheat oven to 350°F (175°C). Wrap tortillas in foil and place in oven for 8–10 minutes. Place 2 cups (500 ml) enchilada sauce in a 10- by 15-inch (25- by 37.5-cm) baking dish.

2. Remove tortillas from oven and unwrap. Spoon ½ cup (125 ml) beans along center of each tortilla. Sprinkle 2 table-spoons cheese over beans. Drizzle with 1 tablespoon enchilada sauce. Roll up, and place enchilada in baking dish. Repeat with remaining tortillas.

3. Sprinkle with remaining cheese. Place in preheated oven until cheese is melted and filling is heated (about 25–30 minutes). Serve on individual plates with salsa on the side. Top each enchilada with a dollop of guacamole.

Makes 12 enchiladas.

Huevos Rancheros in Tortilla Bowls

This Mexican classic is a feast for the eyes as well as the mouth. If you prefer, poach the eggs instead of frying them.

6	tortillas	6
1 can (15 oz)	stewed tomatoes	1 can (430 g)
to taste	hot or mild salsa	to taste
1 can (30 oz)	refried beans	1 can (850 g)
2 tbl	butter	2 tbl
6	eggs	6
1 recipe	Quick Guacamole (see page 33)	1 recipe
as needed	cilantro (coriander leaves), for garnish	as needed

1. Prepare tortilla bowls (see below) and set aside.

2. Place stewed tomatoes in a saucepan and heat over medium heat. Add salsa to taste. Heat refried beans separately.

3. To prepare eggs, heat butter in a 12-inch (30-cm) skillet. Carefully break eggs and add to skillet one at a time. Cook slowly, basting with butter, until white is barely set and yolk is still bright yellow.

4. For each serving, fill a prepared tortilla bowl with ½ cup (125 ml) beans, a cooked egg, ½ cup (125 ml) tomato-salsa mixture, and ⅓ cup guacamole. Garnish with cilantro.

Serves 6.

Making Tortilla Bowls

Flour tortillas baked into fluted bowls can turn a simple dish into something special. To speed up the process, work with 2 or 3 cake pans at a time. Preheat oven to 375°F (190°C). Press a large flour tortilla into an 8-inch (20-cm) round cake pan so that the bottom of the tortilla forms a shallow bowl. Place in preheated oven and bake until slightly crisp (7–10 minutes). Carefully slide from the pan onto a serving dish. Repeat with the remaining tortillas.

FLAUTAS

Flautas (flutes) are corn tortillas that are filled and rolled, then fried. Use tortillas that are at least one day old; freshly made corn tortillas do not fry well. You can overlap two tortillas for extra strength and length. Serve flautas as an appetizer or main dish.

24	day-old corn tortillas	24
1 recipe	Mexican filling (see pages 29–33)	1 recipe
as needed	oil, for frying	as needed
as needed	salt	as needed
as needed	shredded lettuce	as needed
1 recipe	Quick Guacamole (see page 33)	1 recipe
1 recipe	Salsa Verde (see page 34)	1 recipe
as needed	sour cream	as needed

1. Preheat a heavy frying pan or comal over high heat. The pan is sufficiently hot when a drop of water dances when dropped onto the heated surface. Dampen your hands with water and rub the tortilla to moisten. Cook briefly, turning once, only long enough to soften the tortilla.

2. Fill the tortilla with 2–3 tablespoons of the prepared filling. Roll tightly and secure with a toothpick. Set aside and cook and fill the remaining tortillas.

3. Pour oil into a skillet to depth of ½ inch (1.25 cm). Heat over high heat to 400°F (205°C). (Oil is sufficiently hot when a tiny bit of tortilla dropped into it pops immediately to the surface.) Lightly salt the flautas and fry, several at a time, until golden and crisp. Drain on paper towels and remove the toothpicks. Keep fried flautas warm in a 300°F (150°C) oven while the remaining flautas are fried.

4. Mound lettuce on a large platter. Arrange flautas over lettuce. Garnish with guacamole, salsa, and a dollop of sour cream.

Makes 24 flautas.

SIRLOIN FAJITAS

A favorite in the U.S. Southwest, fajitas are made by combining strips of beef or chicken fried with sautéed onions, mushrooms, and chiles, and rolling the mixture into warm flour tortillas. This recipe uses lean sirloin steak strips, sautéed quickly in a serrano chile sauce and garnished with nonfat yogurt and slices of avocado.

1 cup	sliced onions	250 ml
1 cup	sliced mushrooms	250 ml
1 tsp	oil	1 tsp
⅓ cup	dry sherry	85 ml
1 lb	sirloin tips, well-trimmed	450 g
2	serrano or jalapeño chiles, seeded and minced	2
½ tsp	cumin seed	½ tsp
¼ tsp	ground coriander	¼ tsp
1 tsp	minced cilantro (coriander leaves)	1 tsp
4	flour tortillas	4
½ cup	salsa (see page 34)	125 ml
½	avocado, thinly sliced	½
1 cup	nonfat yogurt	250 ml

1. In a large skillet over medium-high heat, sauté onions and mushrooms in oil and sherry for 10 minutes. Cut steak into 1½-inch (3.75-cm) strips and add to sauté, cooking for 2 minutes more. Add chiles, cumin, coriander, and cilantro, and cook 3 more minutes, stirring frequently.

2. Warm tortillas in oven. Set out bowls of salsa, sliced avocado, and yogurt. Wrap warmed tortillas in clean cloth napkin. Serve meat filling from skillet or place in prewarmed serving dish.

Serves 4.

TUCSON CHIMICHANGAS

A chimichanga is Arizona's lusciously overstuffed version of a burrito. Be sure to use freshly made tortillas. Stale tortillas will crack.

1½ cups	shredded cooked turkey or chicken	350 ml
1¼ cups	grated Monterey jack cheese	300 ml
1 can (4 oz)	diced mild green chiles, drained	1 can (115 g)
2	fresh tomatoes, diced	2
2 tbl	minced cilantro (coriander leaves)	2 tbl
½ tsp each	ground cumin, dried oregano, and salt	½ tsp each
2 tbl	oil	2 tbl
2 cloves	garlic, minced	2 cloves
1	onion, minced	1
6	fresh large flour tortillas	6
as needed	oil for deep-frying	as needed
1 recipe	Salsa Verde (see page 34)	1 recipe
1 recipe	Quick Guacamole (see page 33)	1 recipe
2 cups	sour cream, for garnish	500 ml
1 head	lettuce, shredded, for garnish	1 head
2	fresh tomatoes, chopped, for garnish	2
1 can (4 oz)	sliced black olives, for garnish	1 can (115 g)
6	radishes, sliced, for garnish	6

1. In a large bowl combine turkey or chicken, cheese, chiles, tomatoes, cilantro, cumin, oregano, and salt.

2. In a skillet heat oil. Add garlic and onion and sauté over medium heat until wilted (about 5 minutes). Stir into the chicken mixture.

3. In center of each tortilla place a generous spoonful of the chicken mixture, leaving about 2 inches (5 cm) of tortilla uncovered at each end. Fold over both ends, then fold over the sides. Secure with toothpicks. Repeat until all tortillas are filled.

4. In a large, deep skillet, heat an inch (2.5 cm) of oil to 350°F (175°C). Gently place each chimichanga in the oil, seam side

down. Fry until lightly browned and crisp (about 1 minute), then carefully turn and fry the other side. Remove and drain chimichanga on paper towels and keep warm in a low oven. Repeat until all chimichangas are cooked.

5. To serve, place chimichanga on a plate and remove toothpicks. Coat with salsa and top with a dollop of guacamole and sour cream. Garnish with lettuce topped with tomatoes, olives, and radishes.

Serves 6.

Grilled Albacore Tacos

Fresh albacore tuna makes wonderful tacos.

1½–2 lb	albacore fillets or steaks	680–900 g
as needed	olive oil	as needed
as needed	freshly ground black pepper	as needed
as needed	fresh oregano	as needed
12	warm tortillas or taco shells (see below)	12
1 cup	Salsa Verde (see page 34)	250 ml

1. Cut albacore into 1-inch (2.5–cm) cubes. Thread on skewers. Drizzle with olive oil; sprinkle with pepper and oregano. Marinate in refrigerator 1–4 hours, turning occasionally. Remove fish from refrigerator at least 30 minutes before grilling.

2. Build a hot charcoal fire and let it burn down to a red glow. Prepare tortillas (see below) and keep warm. Grill fish over hottest part of fire until just done (3–5 minutes per side). To serve, wrap a skewer of fish in a tortilla, garnish with salsa, and remove skewer.

Serves 4 to 6.

Preparing Tortillas for Tacos

Traditional Method *Heat an ungreased skillet over high heat. Dampen hands with water and rub tortilla to moisten it. Cook, turning once, to soften tortilla. Fill, fold, and serve immediately.*

Fried Method *Heat ¼ inch (.6 cm) oil in skillet to 400°F (205°C). Fry tortilla just long enough to soften. Drain on paper towels. Fill, fold, and serve immediately. For crisp tortillas, use ½ inch (1.25 cm) oil. Fold tortilla in half, holding edges together with tongs. Briefly press center to the bottom of skillet to flatten and set. Turn tortilla on side to cook until golden and crisp. Repeat on other side. Drain on paper towels. Fill and serve immediately.*

Zucchini Quesadillas

A quesadilla is a south-of-the-border grilled cheese sandwich. This straightforward sauté of zucchini and onions makes a terrific luncheon or light supper dish.

3	zucchini	3
1	onion	1
1 tsp	butter or oil	1 tsp
2 cloves	garlic, minced	2 cloves
½ tsp	salt	½ tsp
2 cups	grated jalapeño jack cheese or Monterey jack cheese	500 ml
8	flour tortillas	8

1. Shred zucchini. Slice onion into thin strips. Heat butter or oil in a medium skillet, and sauté onion and garlic until translucent (about 8 minutes). Add zucchini, and cook for about 5 minutes, stirring to mix thoroughly with onion and garlic. Season with salt. Cool slightly.

2. Spread about 3 tablespoons of onion-garlic-zucchini filling over one half of each tortilla, sprinkle with about ⅓ cup (85 ml) grated cheese, and fold tortilla in half. Place 2–3 folded tortillas in a large skillet over medium heat, and heat until cheese is melted.

Serves 4 to 8.

CHILE-CHEESE QUESADILLAS

With a simple filling of melted cheese (Cheddar, Monterey jack, goat cheese, or Brie) layered between two flour tortillas, quesadillas make a quick hors d'oeuvre or accompaniment to soup or salad.

1 cup	grated Cheddar cheese	250 ml
1 cup	grated Monterey jack cheese	250 ml
6	flour tortillas	6
6	green onions, diced	6
¼ cup	diced jalapeño chiles	60 ml
12 sprigs	cilantro (coriander leaves)	12 sprigs
3 tbl	oil	3 tbl
as needed	salsa (see page 34)	as needed

1. In a small bowl combine cheeses. Place 3 tortillas on work surface. Top each with one third of the cheese, green onions, chiles, and cilantro. Cover each tortilla with a second tortilla.

2. In a 10-inch (25 cm) skillet over medium-high heat, heat 1 teaspoon oil. Carefully cook stuffed tortillas, one at a time, until very lightly browned and crispy (about 3 minutes). Carefully turn and cook second side until lightly browned and cheese is melted (about 2 minutes).

3. Remove from pan and reserve in a warm oven until all quesadillas are done. Cut each into wedges and serve with salsa.

Makes 3 quesadillas.

Note *For baked quesadillas, preheat oven to 450°F (230°C). Place 3 tortillas on a baking sheet; top each with one third of the cheese, green onions, chiles, and cilantro. Cover each with a second tortilla. Brush top tortilla with oil and bake until heated throughout (4–7 minutes).*

PACIFIC-RIM QUESADILLAS

Green-onion pancakes, a specialty of Shandong Province, are a favorite item in Chinese restaurants. Sprinkle a bit of cheese over the top and you have an open-face quesadilla.

1 recipe	dough for Mandarin Pancakes (see page 20)	1 recipe
as needed	flour, for dusting	as needed
2–3 tsp	Asian sesame oil	2–3 tsp
as needed	salt	as needed
½ cup	finely minced green onion	125 ml
as needed	oil, for preparing pan	as needed
1 cup	grated Monterey jack cheese	250 ml

1. Prepare dough through kneading and resting stage (step 1). Divide dough in half. Roll 1 piece out on a floured surface to an oblong shape 12–14 inches (30–35 cm) long. Rub a generous teaspoon of sesame oil over the surface of the dough to within 1 inch (2.5 cm) of the edges. Sprinkle evenly with salt, and scatter half the green onion over the surface, again stopping 1 inch (2.5 cm) from the edge.

2. Roll up dough into a log. Coil the rolled dough into a spiral shape and tuck end underneath edge. Roll out coil to a 10-inch (25-cm) circle. Repeat with other piece of dough. (Dough can be prepared to this point and refrigerated or frozen.)

3. Heat a griddle or heavy skillet over medium-low heat. Oil pan generously and cook cakes, one at a time, until covered with brown blisters (about 5 minutes per side). Sprinkle with cheese. Serve hot, cut into wedges.

Makes 2 large quesadillas.

HUNAN TORTILLAS WITH SPICY CARROT SALAD

These cross-cultural tortillas make a simple light meal.

Spicy Carrot Salad

2 cloves	garlic, minced	2 cloves
¼ tsp	hot-pepper flakes	¼ tsp
3 tbl	red wine vinegar	3 tbl
2 tbl	sugar	2 tbl
2 tbl	water	2 tbl
1 tbl	tomato paste	1 tbl
2	carrots, peeled and shredded	2
12	flour tortillas	12
6 tsp	Asian sesame oil	6 tsp
¾ tsp	coarse salt	¾ tsp
6	green onions, minced	6
6 tsp	oil, for frying	6 tsp
as needed	coarse salt, for topping	as needed

1. To prepare Spicy Carrot Salad, place garlic, hot-pepper flakes, vinegar, sugar, water, and tomato paste in a small saucepan. Mix thoroughly and bring mixture to a boil. Place carrots in a mixing bowl. Pour hot sauce over carrots. Let marinate 20 minutes before using. Spicy Carrot Salad will keep in the refrigerator for several days.

2. Brush 6 flour tortillas with ½ teaspoon sesame oil each; sprinkle each with ⅛ teaspoon coarse salt and 1 minced green onion. Top each prepared tortilla with a plain tortilla.

3. In a skillet over medium heat, sauté each pair of tortillas in oil until light and golden brown on first side (about 2 minutes); turn and brown on second side (about 1 minute). Sprinkle top with coarse salt.

4. Cut each double-layered tortilla into wedges and serve warm, topped with Spicy Carrot Salad.

Serves 6.

Mu Shu Pork with Mandarin Pancakes

This Beijing-style dish is one of the most popular selections in restaurants specializing in Mandarin-style dishes. The bamboo shoots, lily buds, cloud ear mushrooms, and hoisin sauce are available in Asian markets. For a multi-ethnic treat, substitute flour tortillas for the pancakes.

3	green onions	3
1 tbl	grated ginger	1 tbl
1 tbl	soy sauce	1 tbl
2 tbl	water	2 tbl
pinch	sugar	pinch
3 tbl	oil	3 tbl
2	eggs, lightly beaten	2
½ lb	lean pork, in matchstick shreds	225 g
¼ cup	shredded bamboo shoots	60 ml
¼ cup	dried lily buds	60 ml
¼ cup	dried cloud ear mushrooms, soaked in warm water and drained	60 ml
8	warm Mandarin Pancakes (see page 20) or flour tortillas	8
¼ cup	bottled hoisin sauce	60 ml

1. Cut white parts of green onions into shreds and combine with ginger. Shred green tops and set aside. Combine soy sauce, water, and sugar; set aside.

2. Heat wok over medium heat. Add 1 tablespoon of the oil and swirl to coat sides of pan. Add eggs and cook just until set. Remove eggs to cutting board and cut into thin strips.

3. Wipe wok clean and return to heat. Heat remaining oil and add ginger-green onion mixture. Stir-fry until fragrant, then add pork. Cook just until pork loses its raw color. Add bamboo shoots, lily buds, and cloud ears; stir-fry 2 minutes longer. Add soy sauce mixture and egg strips, increase heat to high, and cook until nearly all liquid is evaporated. Adjust seasoning and transfer to serving platter.

4. Serve warm Mandarin Pancakes or tortillas on a separate plate, with green-onion shreds and hoisin sauce in small dishes. For each serving, spread a pancake with ½ teaspoon of the sauce, add a few green onion shreds, and top with some of the pork mixture. Roll the pancake around the filling and eat with the fingers.

Serves 4.

Peking Burrito

For this recipe you can buy half a Cantonese roast duck from a Chinese delicatessen or restaurant, and the hot bean sauce, Asian sesame oil, hot chile oil, and black sesame seed at Asian markets.

2 tbl	peanut oil	2 tbl
1 tsp each	minced fresh ginger and garlic	1 tsp each
1 tbl	hot bean sauce	1 tbl
1 cup	thinly sliced carrot, blanched 1 minute	250 ml
1 cup	thinly sliced cabbage	250 ml
1 cup	thinly sliced fresh snow peas	250 ml
2 cups	shredded cooked duck meat with skin	500 ml
2	green onions, shredded	2
½ tsp	sugar	½ tsp
1 tsp	soy sauce, or more as needed	1 tsp
as needed	Asian sesame oil and hot chile oil	as needed
as needed	toasted black sesame seed, for garnish	as needed
8	warm Mandarin Pancakes (see page 20)	8
as needed	cilantro (coriander leaves)	as needed
4 tbl	bottled hoisin sauce	4 tbl

1. Preheat wok over medium-high heat until hot. Pour in peanut oil, then add ginger and garlic and stir-fry until oil is fragrant (about 10 seconds). Add hot bean sauce and cook 5 seconds longer. Increase heat to high. Add carrot, cabbage, and snow peas; stir-fry until cabbage begins to wilt and snow peas turn bright green (about 30 seconds). Add duck, green onions, sugar, and soy sauce; stir-fry until mixture is heated through (about 30 seconds). Add a few drops each sesame oil and hot chile oil. Remove mixture to a serving platter and garnish with sesame seed.

2. To serve, spread 3 tablespoons filling along center of each pancake, add a few sprigs of cilantro, about ½ tablespoon hoisin sauce, and fold pancake around filling.

Serves 4.

LUMPIA LUZON

In this version of lumpia, a Philippine specialty, the cooked filling is first wrapped in a lettuce leaf, then rolled in the spring roll wrapper and eaten without any further cooking. Fresh homemade wrappers are best for this dish (see page 22). You can find bamboo shoots or hearts of palm at Asian markets.

1 recipe	Sweet Lumpia Sauce (see page 38)	1 recipe
16	tender lettuce leaves	16
16	spring roll wrappers (see page 22)	16
1 tbl	oil	1 tbl
3	thick slices bacon, diced and blanched	3
2 tbl	minced garlic	2 tbl
1 cup	finely diced boiling potatoes	250 ml
1	onion, diced	1
½ cup	shredded bamboo shoots or hearts of palm	125 ml
¼ cup	shredded cabbage	60 ml
½ lb	cooked pork or chicken, diced	225 g
¼ lb	cooked shrimp, diced	115 g
to taste	salt and freshly ground black pepper	to taste

1. Prepare Sweet Lumpia Sauce and set aside.

2. Arrange lettuce leaves and wrappers on a platter, with sauce in a bowl alongside.

3. In a wok or skillet, heat oil over medium-low heat and cook bacon until lightly browned. Add garlic and cook until fragrant. Add potatoes and onion and cook until potatoes are tender. Add bamboo shoots or hearts of palm, cabbage, pork or chicken, and shrimp, and stir-fry until mixture is heated through. Season to taste with salt and pepper and transfer to a serving bowl.

4. To serve, spoon filling into the center of a lettuce leaf and add sauce to taste. Roll the leaf in a wrapper, enclosing the filling and the base of the leaf.

Serves 4 to 6 as an appetizer.

LUMPIA SHANGHAI

This Philippine specialty gets its name from the Chinese-style filling; another possibility is to use the filling for Lumpia Luzon (see page 76), but cut the meats and vegetables into smaller pieces and omit the lettuce leaves.

1 recipe	Sweet Lumpia Sauce (see page 38)	1 recipe
½ lb	finely ground pork or beef	225 g
¼ cup	minced green onion	60 ml
1 tbl each	minced ginger and garlic	1 tbl each
4	dried cloud ear mushrooms, soaked, drained, and diced	4
¼ cup	finely diced water chestnuts or jicama	60 ml
1 tbl	bottled fish sauce	1 tbl
1	egg	1
to taste	freshly ground black pepper	to taste
16	spring roll wrappers (see page 22)	16
as needed	oil, for deep frying	as needed

1. Prepare Sweet Lumpia Sauce and set aside.

2. In a bowl, combine pork, green onion, ginger, garlic, mush-rooms, water chestnuts, and fish sauce and blend thoroughly. Beat egg lightly and add to pork mixture, reserving a teaspoon or so for sealing rolls. Season generously with pepper. Sauté a small piece of filling, taste, and adjust seasoning.

3. Spread about 2 tablespoons filling diagonally across the middle of a wrapper. Roll and seal as shown in Preparing Spring Rolls and Lumpia, page 23. Lumpia may be rolled up to 1 hour ahead of frying.

4. Heat oil in fryer to 350°F (175°C). Fry lumpia a few at a time until golden brown; drain on paper towels. Serve immediately or keep warm in oven. Serve with Sweet Lumpia Sauce.

Serves 8 as an appetizer.

Shrimp Pocket Sandwiches

For a quick dinner, pita bread combines a salad and the sandwich filling of your choice.

2 cups	cooked shrimp	500 ml
2 tbl	olive oil	2 tbl
1 tbl	freshly squeezed lemon juice	1 tbl
4	pita breads, halved	4
1 clove	garlic, minced	1 clove
½ cup	mayonnaise	125 ml
8	lettuce leaves	8
1 cup	shredded lettuce	250 ml
8 slices	provolone or mozzarella cheese	8 slices
8 slices each	tomato and cucumber	8 slices each

1. Combine shrimp with olive oil and lemon juice and set aside.

2. Wrap pita bread halves in a dampened towel and warm in 350°F (175°C) oven for 10 minutes.

3. Mix garlic with mayonnaise. Spread inside of pita bread halves with mayonnaise.

4. Place 1 lettuce leaf and 2 tablespoons shredded lettuce in each half; top with 1 slice each cheese, tomato, and cucumber, and add the shrimp filling. Serve at once.

Makes 8 sandwiches.

TURKEY PITA TOSTADAS

A ground turkey filling atop a warm pita with a garnish of cool vegetables and sour cream is just the ticket on a balmy summer night.

1 tbl	butter	1 tbl
1 lb	ground turkey	450 g
½ cup	chopped red onion	125 ml
3–4 tbl	salsa (see page 34)	3–4 tbl
1 tsp	dried oregano	1 tsp
⅛ tsp	ground cumin	⅛ tsp
½ tsp	salt	½ tsp
¼ tsp	freshly ground black pepper	¼ tsp
4	whole pita breads	4
2 cups	shredded lettuce	500 ml
1	avocado, sliced	1
¼ cup	sour cream	60 ml
as needed	additional salsa	as needed
2	tomatoes, cut in wedges	2
8	ripe olives	8

1. In a large frying pan over high heat, melt butter. Add turkey, breaking up with a fork. Add onion, salsa, and spices and cook until turkey is golden and juices are clear.

2. To warm pita breads, wrap in a damp towel and heat in a 350°F (175°C) oven for 10–15 minutes.

3. To assemble each serving, place a whole pita bread on each plate. Top with a quarter of the lettuce, turkey mixture, avocado, sour cream, and salsa. Garnish with tomato and olives.

Makes 4 tostadas.

SRI LANKAN CURRY WITH CHAPATIS

The fruits in this curry soften the bite of the chiles.

2 tbl	olive oil	2 tbl
2 tbl	curry powder	2 tbl
1 tsp	crushed dried hot chiles	1 tsp
8 cloves	garlic, finely minced	8 cloves
2 tbl	grated fresh ginger	2 tbl
3 lb	cooked cubed lamb	1.4 kg
2 cups	beef stock	500 ml
½ cup	brown sugar	125 ml
¼ cup	distilled vinegar	60 ml
4	onions, cut into large chunks	4
2	apples, peeled, cored, and cut into bite-sized chunks	2
2	seedless oranges, sliced with peel intact	2
1½ cups	fresh ripe pineapple, cored and diced	350 ml
1 tbl	cornstarch dissolved in 1 tbl water	1 tbl
as needed	salt and fresh ground black pepper	as needed
½ tbl	minced cilantro (coriander leaves)	½ tbl
1 heaping tbl	minced fresh mint leaves	1 heaping tbl
4	green onions, minced	4
as needed	warm chapatis (see page 24)	as needed

1. Heat the oil over high heat in a large skillet. Add the curry powder, chiles, garlic, and ginger. Cook for about 2 minutes, stirring rapidly. Add the meat and stir to coat evenly. Pour in the stock, reduce heat and simmer until tender (about 15 minutes). Add the brown sugar and vinegar.

2. Add the onion chunks and fruits and continue simmering until the apples are tender. Stir cornstarch mixture into the onion mixture, and simmer, stirring gently, until the sauce is thick and glossy. Add salt and pepper to taste. Add the cilantro, mint, and green onions and stir lightly. Serve with warm chapatis.

Serves 6.

SIK SIK WAT

This spicy beef and pepper stew is of Ethiopian origin.

20 small	dried hot chiles	20 small
2½–3 lb	boneless beef, cubed	1.2–1.4 kg
¼ cup	peanut oil	¼ cup
10–12 cloves	garlic, minced	10–12 cloves
2	onions, sliced	2
4	small fresh hot chiles, seeded and sliced	4
1 tbl	grated fresh ginger	1 tbl
¼ tsp	ground fenugreek	¼ tsp
½ tsp	ground cinnamon	½ tsp
¼ tsp each	ground nutmeg, cardamom, and coriander	¼ tsp each
2 tbl	paprika	2 tbl
¼ cup	Berberé Sauce (see page 39)	60 ml
2	chopped tomatoes	2
½ cup	dry red wine	125 ml
⅓–½ cup	sugar	85–125 ml
to taste	coarsely ground black pepper and salt	to taste
2	lemons, cut into wedges, for garnish	2
8–10	chapatis or flour tortillas	8–10

1. Put dried chiles into a medium bowl and add boiling water to cover. Soak for 1 hour, drain, and repeat process. Set aside.

2. Brown beef in hot oil in a large, heavy pan over moderate heat until beef is seared. Remove and set aside. Add garlic, onions, and fresh chiles, and sauté until soft but not browned (2–3 minutes). Add fresh ginger, spices, and Berberé Sauce, and cook, stirring constantly, for 2 minutes. Add tomatoes, wine, sugar and pepper and salt to taste. Stir and reduce heat. Simmer until beef is very tender (1–1½ hours), stirring occasionally. Taste and adjust seasonings about halfway through cooking.

3. Garnish with lemon wedges and serve with chapatis or tortillas.

Serves 8.

MIXED VEGETABLE CRÊPES

A quick vegetable sauté makes a fast supper or lunch dish when you wrap it into a crêpe (or a tortilla).

2 tbl	butter	2 tbl
6 tbl	minced shallot	6 tbl
3 cups	coarsely grated zucchini	700 ml
¾ cup	coarsely grated carrot	175 ml
½ cup	toasted pine nuts	125 ml
¼ cup	balsamic vinegar	60 ml
to taste	salt and freshly ground black pepper	to taste
8	Basic Crêpes (see page 26)	8
as needed	melted butter, for garnish	as needed

1. In a large skillet over moderate heat, melt butter. Add shallot and sauté 1 minute. Add zucchini and carrot and sauté until wilted, about 3 minutes. Add pine nuts and vinegar and cook 30 seconds. Add salt and pepper. Vegetables may be sautéed up to 1 day in advance and refrigerated; undercook vegetables slightly if they will be reheated. Reheat quickly over high heat before using.

2. To serve, spoon about ¼ cup (60 ml) of filling down the center of each crêpe and roll or fold like an envelope. Brush rolled crêpes with a little melted butter, for garnish, and serve at once.

Makes 8 crêpes.

Ratatouille Crêpes

These crêpes are rolled around a savory, mildly spicy filling of tomatoes, eggplant, and bell peppers. This delightful and tasty dish combines the classic flavors of two Gallic specialties: ratatouille, the famous vegetable stew of Provence, and crêpes, French pancakes.

2 tbl	olive oil	2 tbl
2 cups	chopped eggplant	500 ml
1	onion, sliced thinly	1
1 clove	garlic, minced	1 clove
2	red bell peppers, seeded and chopped coarsely	2
2	zucchini, sliced into rounds	2
3	tomatoes, cored and chopped coarsely	3
1 tbl	chopped fresh basil	1 tbl
12	Basic Crêpes (see page 26)	12
½ cup	grated Monterey jack cheese	125 ml

1. Heat oil in a skillet until fragrant. Add eggplant, onion, garlic, bell peppers, zucchini, tomatoes, and basil. Cook over medium heat until soft (about 25 minutes).

2. To assemble crêpes, spoon ½ cup (125 ml) of ratatouille vegetable mixture into the center of each crêpe; roll and place seam side down in a baking dish. Sprinkle crêpes with cheese and broil until cheese melts. Serve hot.

Serves 6.

DESSERTS

Among internationally famous wrappers, tortillas and crêpes are especially well suited to the dessert course. Mild-flavored flour tortillas are an ideal medium for sugar and spice, and sweet crêpes with a variety of fillings have long been a favorite of French cuisine. Use the recipes and ideas in this section to launch a dessert buffet with an assortment of wrapped and filled sweets.

ICE CREAM TOSTADAS

Try this for a cool, crunchy ending to your next Mexican meal.

Cinnamon Ice Cream

1 qt	vanilla ice cream, softened	900 ml
2 tbl	ground cinnamon	2 tbl

Apple Purée

3 lb	apples, peeled and cored	1.4 kg
½ cup	unsalted butter	125 ml
1 cup	sugar	250 ml
3 tbl	lemon juice	3 tbl
½ tsp	ground cinnamon	½ tsp
¼ tsp	freshly grated nutmeg	¼ tsp
2 tbl	Calvados or applejack	2 tbl

8	Cinnamon Buñuelas, whole (see page 94)	8
1 qt	chocolate ice cream	900 ml
1 cup	bottled chocolate sauce	250 ml

1. To prepare Cinnamon Ice Cream, combine softened vanilla ice cream with cinnamon and refreeze.

2. To prepare Apple Purée, place all ingredients in a 2½-quart (2.3-l) saucepan. Cover and cook over medium heat, stirring occasionally, until apples are soft (about 25 minutes). Purée in a food processor or blender. Set aside and keep warm.

3. To assemble, spoon about ½ cup (125 ml) Apple Purée along one side of each dessert plate. Place a warm Cinnamon Buñuela on the other side of the plate. Place 1 scoop each Cinnamon Ice Cream and chocolate ice cream on top of the buñuela and drizzle about 2 tablespoons of sauce on top. Serve immediately.

Serves 8.

Honey-Pear-Butter Crêpes

The pear butter can be made up to two days in advance and refrigerated. If mixture separates, return to food processor and process briefly to reblend. See photo on page 87.

Honey-Pear Butter

1 cup	very ripe pear, peeled, cored, and cubed	250 ml
1 cup	butter, softened	150 ml
¼ cup	honey	60 ml
½ recipe	Basic Crêpes, with 1 tbl sugar added to the batter (see page 26)	½ recipe

1. To prepare Honey-Pear Butter, place pear in a food processor or blender and blend until puréed. Add butter and honey and process until completely smooth.

2. Cook Basic Crêpes, following instructions on page 27.

3. To assemble, spread about 1½ tablespoons Honey-Pear Butter evenly over surface of each hot crêpe; fold crêpes in quarters and serve immediately.

Makes 8 crêpes.

CRÊPE DESSERTS

A stack of freshly made dessert crepes and an assortment of sweet fillings translate into an instant dessert buffet. Use the Basic Crêpe recipe on page 26, adding 2 tablespoons granulated or brown sugar to the liquid ingredients.

Fresh Fruit Crêpes *Fill dessert crêpes with whatever sliced fresh fruits are in season (raspberries, strawberries, blueberries, peaches, nectarines, kiwi fruit, bananas, etc.). Roll and top with preserves and a dollop of yogurt or sour cream.*

Ice Cream Crêpes *Spoon small scoops of softened vanilla ice cream down the center of a dessert crêpe. Fold in the sides and drizzle with hot chocolate sauce.*

Jam-Filled Crêpes *Spread dessert crêpe with strawberry jam, apple butter, or other fruit preserves. Fold in quarters and drizzle with crème fraîche, sour cream, or yogurt.*

Lemon-Honey-Butter Crêpes *Combine ½ cup (125 ml) softened unsalted butter, 1 teaspoon grated lemon zest, 2 tablespoons lemon juice, and 3 tablespoons honey and blend until smooth. Put a dab of Lemon-Honey Butter on dessert crêpe and drizzle with crème fraîche.*

Maple Syrup Crêpes *Top dessert crêpe with melted butter, warm maple syrup, and chopped walnuts.*

Orange-Honey-Butter Crêpes *Blend ½ cup (125 ml) softened unsalted butter with 3 tablespoons honey and 1 teaspoon grated orange zest to taste. Put a dab of Orange-Honey Butter on crêpe and drizzle with crème fraîche.*

Sweet Cheese-Filled Crêpes *Spread dessert crêpe with 1 tablespoon softened cream cheese. Fold in quarters and drizzle with honey or hot fudge sauce.*

Cinnamon Buñuelas

These Mexican "cookies" made from fried tortillas make a wonderful snack or the base for recipes like the Ice Cream Tostadas featured on page 91. If you use store-bought flour tortillas, you can use a small bowl as a guide and cut around the rim to trim the tortillas to a smaller size.

1 tbl	ground cinnamon	1 tbl
4 tbl	sugar	4 tbl
8	small flour tortillas	8
as needed	oil, for frying	as needed

1. In a small bowl combine cinnamon and sugar; set aside.

2. Cut each tortillas into 6 wedges or leave whole for Ice Cream Tostadas (page 91).

3. In a large skillet heat about ½ inch (1.25 cm) oil over medium-high heat. Fry tortillas, turning once, until they are golden (about 1 minute). Transfer tortillas to paper towels to drain. Sprinkle with cinnamon-sugar mixture.

Makes 48 wedges or 8 whole buñuelas.

Index

Note: Page numbers in italics refer to illustrations.

Basic Crêpes 26
Beef
    New Mexico-Style Burritos 48,
        49
    Sirloin Fajitas 60, *61*
    Lumpia Shanghai 78, *79*
    Machaca Filling 30
    Picadillo Filling *28*, 29
    Sik Sik Wat 85
Berberé Sauce 39
Breads and wrappers
    Basic Crêpes 26
    Chapatis 8, 24
    Corn Tortillas 6, 13
    Flour Tortillas 6, *12*, 16
    Making Corn and Flour Tortillas
        14–15
    Making Crêpes 27
    Making Sopes 19
    Making Tortilla Bowls 56
    Mandarin Pancakes 7, 20, *21*
    Pita Bread 25
    *Preparing Spring Rolls and
        Lumpia* 23
    Preparing Tortillas for Tacos 64
    Sopes 17, *18*
    Spring Roll Wrappers I 22
    Spring Roll Wrappers II 22
Brown Bag Tortillas 30

Chapatis 8, 24
Cheese and Bacon Crêpes 42
Chicken Mole Torta 46, *47*
Chicken-Liver Crêpes 42
Chicken-Tomatillo Filling 32
Chile-Cheese Quesadillas 66, *67*
Cinnamon Buñuelas 94
Corn Tortillas 6, *12*, 13
Crêpes, about 8
    Basic 26
    Crêpe Desserts 93
    Making Crêpes 27
    Savory Crêpe Fillings 42
Crêpe Desserts 93

Enchiladas Coloradas 52, *53*
Ensenada Enchiladas 54, *55*

Fish and shellfish
    Grilled Albacore Tacos 64
    Lumpia Luzon 76, *77*
    Pescado Filling 33
    Shrimp Burritos Cancún 50, *51*
    Shrimp Pocket Sandwiches 80,
        81
    Spicy Crabmeat Tostadas *44*, 45
Flautas 58, *59*
Flour Tortillas 6, *12*, 16
Fresh Fruit Crêpes 93

Garnishes for Tacos and Sopes 17
Greek Salad Filling 40, *41*
Grilled Albacore Tacos 64

Ham and Cheese Crêpes 42
Honey-Pear-Butter Crêpes 92
Huevos Rancheros in Tortilla Bowls
    56, *57*
Hummus 41
Hunan Tortillas with Spicy Carrot
    Salad 70, *71*

Ice Cream Crêpes 93
Ice Cream Tostadas *90*, 91
Imperial Asian Filling 37

Jam-Filled Crêpes 93

Lemon-Honey-Butter Crêpes 93
Lumpia Luzon 76, *77*
Lumpia Shanghai 78, *79*

Machaca Filling 30
Making Corn and Flour Tortillas
    14–15
Making Crêpes 27
Making Sopes 19
Making Tortilla Bowls 56
Mandarin Pancakes 7, 20, *21*
Maple Syrup Crêpes 93
Mexican Crêpes 42
Mixed Vegetable Crêpes 86, *87*
Mu Shu Pork with Mandarin
    Pancakes 72, *73*
Mushroom Crêpes 42

New Mexico-Style Beef Burritos 48,
    49
Nuoc Mam Sauce 38, *39*

Orange-Honey-Butter Crêpes 93

Pacific-Rim Quesadillas 68, *69*
Peking Burrito 74, *75*
Pescado Filling 33
Picadillo Filling *28*, 29
Pita Bread 8, 25
Pork and lamb
    Cheese and Bacon Crêpes 42
    Ham and Cheese Crêpes 42
    Imperial Asian Filling 37
    Lumpia Luzon 76, 77
    Lumpia Shanghai 78, *79*
    Mu Shu Pork with Mandarin
        Pancakes 72, *73*
    Puerco Filling 31
    Sausage and Spinach Crêpes
        42, *43*
    Savory Crêpe Fillings 42
    Spring Roll or Lumpia Filling 36
    Sri Lankan Curry with Chapatis
        84
Poultry
    Chicken Mole Torta 46, *47*
    Chicken-Tomatillo Filling 32
    Lumpia Luzon 76, 77
    Peking Burrito 74, *75*
    Tucson Chimichangas 62, *63*
    Turkey Pita Tostadas 82, *83*
Preparing Spring Rolls and Lumpia
    23
Preparing Tortillas for Tacos 64
Princess Crêpes 42
Provençale Crêpes 42
Puerco Filling 31

Quick Guacamole 33, *35*

Ratatouille Crêpes 88, *89*
Roasting and Peeling Chiles 32

Salad
    Greek Salad Filling 40, *41*
    Spicy Carrot 70
Salsa Azteca 34, *35*
Salsa Verde 34
Sauces and salsas
    Berberé Sauce 39
    Nuoc Mam Sauce 38, *39*
    Quick Guacamole 33, *35*
    Salsa Azteca 34, *35*
    Salsa Verde 34
    Sweet Lumpia Sauce 38
    The Well-Sauced Tortilla 37

Sausage and Spinach Crêpes 42, *43*
Savory Crêpe Fillings 42
Shrimp Burritos Cancún 50, *51*
Shrimp Pocket Sandwiches 80, *81*
Sik Sik Wat 85
Sirloin Fajitas 60, *61*
Smoked Salmon Crêpes 42
Sopes 17, *18*
Spicy Crabmeat Tostadas *44*, 45
Spring Roll or Lumpia Filling 36
Spring Roll Wrappers, about 8
Spring Roll Wrappers I 22
Spring Roll Wrappers II 22
Sri Lankan Curry with Chapatis 84
Sweet Cheese-Filled Crêpes 93
Sweet Lumpia Sauce 38

Tortillas, about 6
    Corn 6, 13
    Flour 6, *12*, 16
    Making 14–15
    Making Tortilla Bowls 56
Tucson Chimichangas 62, *63*
Turkey Pita Tostadas 82, *83*

Well-Sauced Tortilla, The 37

Zucchini Quesadillas 65